URBAN
WILDLIFE HABITATS

BY

BARBARA TAYLOR

LIVING ON THE WILD SIDE

Flocks of pigeons flutter around a city square; the eyes of a fox shine in car headlights; mice scuttle around under the floorboards – three examples of wild animals that share our urban environment. There are many different urban creatures. Some are visible and others are hidden, but all take advantage of urban living. There are many benefits of urban life to the animals – food all year round, warmer temperatures in winter and a variety of places to live. Urban animals have to be adaptable to survive constant change, noise, light, pollution, and of course, people. Some of the animals that adapt to urban living do so too well, and become pests or health hazards.

HIGH-RISE NESTS

White storks normally nest in tall trees but chimneys, church spires and power pylons work just as well. In some European towns, people have built special platforms on their chimneys, so the storks can build their nests there. The storks are supposed to bring good fortune and many babies to those people lucky enough to have a nest on their roof. Sadly though, stork numbers have been falling.

CATS GONE WILD

In many cities there are enormous populations of feral cats. These are domestic cats that have been abandoned or made homeless because of war, fire or floods. Feral cats are independent, secretive and nocturnal, living in factories, warehouses and sewers. They hunt birds, rats and mice. Without them, the problem of urban rats and mice would be more serious.

NESTING SITES

Swallows, swifts and house martins originally lived in caves or on cliff-faces and now nest in buildings. A swallow's nest is usually built on a high ledge. The saucer-shaped nest is made from mud and dried grasses, lined with feathers and bits of plants. Swallows also rest on artificial perches, such as telegraph poles and wires, rather than natural perches, such as trees.

SUPER SURVIVORS

Rats and mice thrive in the heart of cities all over the world. Thousands of brown rats like this one live beneath us in sewers, drains and other underground tunnels. Black rats originally lived in trees and are good climbers. Now they make their home in peoples roofs. Rats and mice first spread to urban habitats by travelling on ships from one port to another.

POPULAR PIGEONS?

Pigeons are rock and cliff-dwelling birds that now make their homes up high in our cities. One of the reasons they survive so well in the urban environment is because they can breed all year round. Some people like the pigeons so much that they feed them – although not always from their own mouths! In Roman times, pigeons were so highly regarded that slaves had to chew bread before it was given to the pigeons. Today, they cause many problems in towns because of the mess they make and the diseases they carry.

ROAD SAFETY

Deciding when to cross a road is a terrifying prospect for many urban animals. Common toads set off to find their breeding ponds in spring but often find a road is now in the way.

AMERICAN CITIES

From cold and snowy Canada to the tropical warmth of Brazil, a large variety of wild animals have made their homes in American cities. Polar bears scavenge around rubbish dumps in icy Canadian towns, while moose sometimes wander through the streets. Peregrine falcons nest on skyscrapers in Los Angeles, swifts nest in factory chimneys, and caimans live in the canal systems of Florida. In some South American cities, house mice with very thick fur even survive in cold, refrigerated warehouses. But American cities also have plenty of the most common city birds – the house sparrow, the feral pigeon and the starling. They are not native birds but were introduced at different times – pigeons in the 17th century, sparrows between 1850 and 1870, and starlings in 1890-91, when a flock of 100 birds were released into Central Park, New York. Today, there are over 50 million starlings in North America.

GARDEN PEST

Rabbits such as this eastern cottontail rabbit have become pests in some parts of America. The bunnies eat away at garden plants and dig up the flowerbeds. They are difficult to catch because their large ears help them to detect danger, and their long legs are adapted for fast running. They are good at burrowing and gnawing and often find a way through rabbit-proof fencing.

SUN-BATHING SLOTH

Sloths are one species of animal living in a city park in Santa Cruz, Bolivia. This one seems to be enjoying the sunshine since sloths regulate their body temperature by moving in and out of the sun. It is not frightened of being so close to people. When wild animals are fed regularly by people, they can become very tame.

HAPPY HUMMERS

Hummingbirds are not scared of people so they have no problem living in cities. People in North America often hang hummingbird feeders in their back yards because they enjoy watching the tiny birds. Inside the feeders is a sugary liquid, a lot like the nectar hummingbirds take from flowers. Sugar is a good food for hummingbirds because it can be turned into energy very quickly and hummingbirds need a lot of instant energy to keep their tiny bodies warm and keep flying.

DEER LUNCH

Some wapiti deer seem to find these playing fields a good spot for a rest and a grassy lunch. Urban areas can provide deer with safe refuges from hunters, although such large animals are not common in towns.

PEREGRINE PERCHES

City centres are ideal for peregrine falcons because the tall buildings are just like the rocky cliffs on which they like to breed. There are also plenty of pigeons to eat. In the USA, many young birds bred in captivity have been introduced to cities such as Washington, Baltimore, Cincinnati, Cleveland and Los Angeles. Humans act as surrogate parents, supervising and feeding the birds until they can look after themselves. About a dozen chicks need to be released over two years to ensure one breeding pair. Dangers such as plate-glass windows and wires cause the death of eight out of ten of the young birds.

SKUNK STINK

In American towns after dusk, skunks come out to scavenge for food. But a skunk's black-and-white stripes carry a warning that no one should ignore. To defend itself, a skunk squirts out a ghastly-smelling fluid from its anal glands. Anyone who gets this on their clothes while trying to chase a skunk off their property might as well throw their clothes away – although tomato juice is supposed to reduce the time that the smell lasts.

A hedgehog finds a garden in the suburbs very similar to its natural habitat in the woodlands. It has the same sort of food, such as worms, slugs, snails, beetles and caterpillars, as well as leaves and grasses for nesting with. Unfortunately, there are a lot of hazards for city hedgehogs. Ponds with smooth sides may be impossible to climb out of and autumn bonfires may accidentally be started on top of hibernating hedgehogs.

FEATHERED HUNTERS

Owls, such as the ghostly white barn owl (left), the tawny owl and the little owl, take advantage of the many rodents scurrying about towns, offering them an easy meal. Barn owls have even nested in the cathedral of Notre Dame in Paris. The snoring and hissing of barn owls in church towers may have been partly responsible for stories of ghosts roaming about the churchyards at night.

BUTTERFLY BONANZA

The butterfly bush, *Buddleja davidii*, was introduced from China to Europe and North America as a garden shrub about 100 years ago. Now it thrives on town building sites, as well as in town gardens. Its flowers are extremely attractive to over 20 species of butterfly, such as these peacocks, as well as other nectar-feeding insects, such as hoverflies and bumble bees.

EUROPEAN CITIES

Europe is a busy place. In many European countries, large numbers of people are crowded into noisy towns and cities. The European climate is cold in the far north and warmer in the south. Elk have wandered into the snowy city of Moscow, yet in some towns in warm southern France, the buzzing of semi-tropical cicadas fills the air. Some urban animals have spread eastwards from Europe to other parts of the world. Rabbits and starlings, for example, live in great numbers in Australia. Others have moved in the opposite direction – collared doves spread across Europe from Turkey and brown rats travelled west from their habitats in Russia. European scavengers, such as kites and ravens, have all but disappeared, as towns and cities are cleaner than they used to be. There is, however, still one famous group of ravens kept at the Tower of London.

PIGEON ESCAPES

The hordes of feral pigeons that live in all cities, from London's Trafalgar Square to the Blue Mosque in Afghanistan, are the descendants of domesticated birds raised as a source of food.

They were first domesticated in Iraq over 6,000 years ago. Some city pigeons may also have come from racing pigeons that became lost. Feral pigeons come in a variety of different colours and markings, due partly to breeding and partly as an adaptation to the towns they live in. Dark coloured birds may survive better in colder climates, as dark colours absorb the sun's warmth. Lighter coloured birds stay cooler in warmer climates, as light reflects the heat.

GREY INVADERS

The grey squirrel is a North American species that was introduced to Britain over 100 years ago to give local gentleman something to shoot. About 30 additional introductions followed, leading to a population explosion of grey squirrels. Sadly, this meant the decline of the red squirrel. Grey squirrels love to chew and can cause serious problems if they get inside houses.

ASIAN & AUSTRALIAN CITIES

SCARY SPIDERS

The Sydney funnel-web spider is one of the most dangerous spiders in the world. They live in an area about 160 km (100 miles) from the centre of Sydney. Females do not move far from their burrows but may bite people while they are gardening. Males sometimes enter houses in summer when searching for females and may crawl into shoes or clothing left on the floor. Both sexes are very aggressive and their massive fangs can go through a child's fingernail.

The urban animals of southern Asia and Australia are drawn to the cities for the shelter and the excellent supplies of food. In India, certain animals, such as cows and monkeys, are protected for religious reasons, while jackals, vultures and kites scavenge for leftovers. Some house dwellers, such as the house gecko, are welcome for clearing the rooms of insect pests. Geckos are also considered lucky animals. Others, such as deadly poisonous spiders or snakes are widely feared. Australian city wildlife is dominated by marsupials, such as possums, which nest in lofts. There are also a number of urban species that were introduced to Australia from Europe, such as starlings, sparrows and rabbits. In turn, foxes, stoats and weasels were introduced in the 19th century to stop rabbit numbers getting too high. They were unsuccessful, but are still living in Australia today.

TEMPLE MONKEYS

Monkeys, such as these sitting on the Monkey Temple in Nepal, are treated well by Hindus because of the Hindu monkey god, Hanuman. According to religious texts, the monkey chieftain Hanuman helped the god Vishnu to rescue his wife who was abducted by the demon king Ravana. There are probably more monkeys living in the cities in India than in the forests.

POSSUM LODGERS

In Australian cites, such as
Sydney and Melbourne,
cat-sized common brushtail
possums have invaded homes in large numbers.
This mother and young are nesting in a boarded-
up fireplace. They also get into lofts, where they
sometimes rip up ceilings to make homes. These
possums also raid litter bins and bird-feeders
in suburban gardens.

SACRED COWS

Cows like this are allowed
to wander freely through the
streets of Indian cities and
even raid vegetable stalls.
Hindus respect animal life
and believe that when we
hurt living things, we hurt
ourselves. Many Hindus are
vegetarians. They also think
of cows, which give people
milk to drink, as mothers,
and they never eat beef.

MEGABATS

Fruit bats have furry, fox-like faces and so are also called flying foxes.
They roost in trees during the day and sometimes strip away leaves so
the members of the colony can see each other more clearly. At dusk
they leave their roosts in search of food. In cities such as
Sydney, they feed on the fig trees in the city parks
at night and can often be heard making
harsh, squealing noises.

STREETWISE
KANGAROO

Hopping along a
street in Queensland,
Australia, are a mother
and joey eastern grey
kangaroo. The mother has
only one young at a time and
the young leave the pouch when they
are about 10 months old. Since the late 18th century,
human towns and cities have brought dramatic changes to the
kangaroo's natural habitat, forcing them to compete for land and cope
with predators, such as domestic cats, dogs and European red foxes.

AFRICAN CITIES

Temperatures in African cities are usually high, night and day, except in a few mountainous areas. Rainfall varies a good deal, from the dry northern cities, such as Cairo, to the wet southern cities, such as Cape Town. European starlings were first introduced into Africa in Cape Town in the 19th century. Since then, they have rapidly spread to other places. There are also tropical birds, such as weaverbirds scavenging for leftovers and sunbirds flitting about parks and gardens. Geckos have a useful role eating insects in buildings. But people in Egyptian towns used to be scared of the lobe-footed gecko. This gecko was thought, incorrectly, to spread the terrible disease leprosy, and was even called 'the father of leprosy'. Termites can also be bad news because of the damage they cause to wooden buildings. African city mammals include rats and monkeys, which can be a considerable nuisance.

TAME BIRD

The African pied wagtail is a very tame bird that lives close to human dwellings. It lives in pairs or small groups and has a pleasant song rather like that of a canary. This wagtail nests in holes in buildings and river banks, laying three eggs with many pale, yellowish-brown markings.

CAMP FOLLOWER

This African elephant has wandered into a tourist camp in the Masai Mara National Park in Kenya. Elephants are intelligent animals and they soon learn that human camps are useful sources of extra food or water. Sometimes, camps are built across the migration routes of elephants. Because they are such huge animals, they are difficult to keep out of the camps and may cause damage with their huge size. But for the tourists, the chance to get really close to a wild elephant is an amazing experience. Other wild animals can get too close for comfort. In 1898-99, the man-eating lions of Tsavo stopped all work on the Mombasa to Uganda railroad when workers refused to continue until they were protected. The lions had killed 135 men before they were finally shot.

ROOF-TOP MONKEYS

Colobus monkeys are good climbers and jumpers – their long hair and tails act as parachutes when they leap. In the forests, they rarely climb down to the ground, so getting onto this Kenyan rooftop must have been easy for them. They may be looking for leaves to eat in the garden around the house.

VULTURE DUTY

Walking about with their characteristic 'goose step', Egyptian vultures search for morsels of food among the town and city rubbish dumps of North, Central and East Africa. These vultures also feed on human excrement. The Egyptian vulture is one of the few tool-using birds, breaking eggs by throwing stones onto them.

PETROL ATTENDANT

This yellow baboon looks as if it is waiting to serve petrol to a customer. It may be waiting for a car to arrive in the hope of a free snack. This is a large, slender baboon, which reaches lengths of up to 102 cm (over 3 ft) and has conspicuously long legs. It comes out during the day and lives in groups.

THE ULTIMATE URBAN ANIMAL

Red foxes are common worldwide. They are widespread and numerous in urban Britain, but also live in other cities of Europe, Australia and North America. Foxes have adapted well to city living because they are not very fussy about where they live or what they eat. They are small enough not to be noticed, yet large enough to travel long distances in search of food.

Some foxes live in the country but come into town at night to eat. Urban areas provide foxes with refuge from hunters and traps. Other urban members of the dog family include dingoes, jackals and coyotes.

AMERICAN FOXES

This red fox has set up home in a Colorado cemetery. In North America, urban red foxes have to compete with raccoons, coyotes, bobcats and even cougars. They have not become such familiar urban animals as they have in countries such as Britain.

Adult foxes moult their fur once each year, between spring and mid-summer. While moulting, they often look scruffy, thin and long-legged. In winter, they grow thick, warm coats.

Most urban foxes lead short lives – 55 per cent die in their first year and 80 per cent die before they are three years old. A few lucky animals may survive to live and breed for up to eight years.

Foxes have keen hearing to detect the rustling noises made by voles and other rodents as they move.

Touch-sensitive whiskers and hairs on the muzzle, around the eyes and under the chin help the fox to find its way through vegetation or explore new runs or holes.

FOX SPEAK

To most city dwellers, it is the eerie, blood-chilling screams of foxes in the middle of the night that are most familiar. It is generally the vixens (females) that scream, while the dog foxes bark. These strange noises can be heard at any time of year but are more common in January, when foxes are mating.

TRACKING FOXES

To build up a picture of the number of foxes in towns and cities and how they move about, scientists study their tracks and droppings.

FOX: FRONT FOOT **FOX: BACK FOOT** **DOG**

Fox footprints are like those of a small dog, only narrower. Claw marks are usually clearly visible.

FRESH (DARK)

DRY (WHITE)

Fox droppings are about 7–10 cm (3–4 inches) long. They look like dog droppings but have a twisted point at one end. They are usually dark and may be made up of bits of mice, birds, hard parts of insects, fruit and berries. Older droppings become paler and much more brittle.

Foxes have 42 teeth, including four sharp, pointed canines to kill and tear prey, and carnassial teeth in the side of the mouth for cutting food.

Foxes are relatively small animals, only a little heavier than a pet cat.

DINGO DOGS

The original dingo was a primitive dog that is probably descended from the Indian wolf. It was spread through east Asia by traders and travellers and apparently arrived in Australia some 4,000–6,000 years ago. Today's dingoes breed freely with feral dogs and few pure dingo populations remain. Dingoes scavenge on rubbish heaps but have a wide and varied diet.

CITY COYOTE

In some of the western cities of the United States coyotes have adapted well to urban life. They are particularly common in Los Angeles, where they hide in scrub-filled ravines during the day and move into built-up areas to feed at night. Coyotes can breed with domestic dogs to produce 'coydogs', which are more likely to attack domestic animals, such as cats, dogs and chickens. Coyotes have even attacked people, which is one thing that urban foxes never do.

DAY-TIME VISITORS

MOLE MOUNTAINS

Moles can make a real mess of a grassy lawn in a garden or town park and they are very difficult to get rid of. The molehills we see above ground are the waste soil that they push above ground as they dig their tunnels. Most of their food comes from soil animals, such as worms that fall into their tunnels. In places where food is scarce, moles have to dig more burrows and push up more molehills to find enough food to eat.

Different urban animals are active at different times – some by day and some by night. This helps them to share the food of the urban habitat and avoid competition. Day-time creatures, such as squirrels, are the ones we are most likely to notice, although the night is usually a busier time because most of the people are out of the way. People are the biggest nuisance for urban animals. They swat houseflies, flick away the cobwebs of house spiders and chase squirrels and wasps away from their picnics. The residents of Tokyo swatted about 117 million houseflies on National Fly Day in 1933. People also prevent larger animals from getting in the way of their daily lives, by building fences around their golf courses or killing off populations if they become a problem. But one of the reasons that urban animals survive is that they are not easily frightened by people.

SUPERMARKET SHOP

Great egrets aren't normally supermarket shoppers but they sometimes search supermarket car parks for a free meal of meat scraps. Great egrets usually feed in swamps and marshes, stalking fish, frogs, snakes and crayfish in shallow water. As people have invaded its natural habitat, the great egret has been forced to change some of its feeding habits.

KANGAROO GOLFERS

These kangaroos have taken advantage of this empty Australian golf course to grab a tasty grass snack. It is difficult to make such areas kangaroo-proof, as kangaroos are good at jumping fences and can leap 3 metres (9.5 ft) in height and 9 metres (29.5 ft) in length. Normally, kangaroos graze during the cool night and rest in the shade during the hot day.

FREE FOOD

Grey squirrels will eat almost anything, from garden bulbs, fish, honey and fruit to fungi, carrion and young birds and their eggs. They take full advantage of any free takeaways people leave out for them. Grey squirrels are agile and alert animals with a good sense of smell and very good eyesight. They spend a good deal of time foraging on the ground and have to be always ready to spring into the trees at the first sign of danger.

STRIPED ANGEL

People are usually afraid of wasps because they can sting, but they are in fact very helpful insects. For most of the summer they hunt insect pests in the garden and are far too busy getting food for their young to bother us. At the end of the summer, a wasp colony starts to break up. The workers have no more young to feed and start to turn their attention to fruit and other sweet substances. This is when the wasps can be annoying, but as soon as the weather turns cold, they die. Only the mated queens survive the winter.

A NIGHT ON THE TOWN

W hen the sun sets and people settle down inside their homes for the night, a whole new group of animals emerges from their day-time hiding places. Animal sounds are easier to hear at night because there is less traffic – the hoot of an owl, the snuffling of a badger, the rustling of a raccoon, the fluttering of a moth or the scream of a fox. Many small animals find it easier to hide from their enemies in the darkness. Night-time animals have keen senses, especially of hearing and smell, to help them search for food or mates or detect danger. Animals that lose water easily, such as slugs, snails and woodlice, prefer to come out at night because the air is cooler and damper. In some countries in the spring, a dawn chorus ends the night, as the birds all sing to lay claim to their nesting territory.

BADGER VISIT

Badgers often visit towns for food, but more because the town has spread into their bit of countryside rather than because they have moved into town. They need open space and peace and quiet and are not as adaptable as many urban animals, except in their diet. Badgers eat many things. They love earthworms but will also eat carrion, insects, small mammals and birds, fruit, vegetables and seeds. They have even been seen crunching glass bottles and chewing golf balls.

SUPER MICE

House mice can live almost anywhere – in coal mines, underground stations or even frozen meat stores. They have good eyesight and a particularly good sense of smell. They can also run fast, which is possibly the best defence against their biggest predator – the cat. House mice usually live in extended families with a dominant male, his group of females and several generations of their offspring. One female mouse can have about 25 young in a year. As well as eating our food, house mice can be a problem because they spread diseases and even set off burglar alarms as they patter around the house at night.

CITIZEN RACCOON

The street-wise raccoon not only tolerates people but seems to thrive in dense human settlements such as towns and cities in North America. Generally shy by nature, raccoons visit when humans are fewer, rubbish is fresher and bird tables are fully stocked. They may build their dens in chimneys or drains, which are like the hollow branches or tree trunks in which they nest in the wild. Raccoons succeed at urban life because they are secretive, adaptable and are able to make a meal out of most natural and artificial city foodstuffs. A city can also be a refuge for raccoons, as they may be trapped and hunted in the countryside.

TOAD TRAVELLER

In 1935, some 62,000 South American cane toads were released into Queensland, Australia in an attempt to control sugar-cane pests. The toads spread to many other areas, including residential ones, and began to eat useful creatures, such as geckos and small frogs. Cane toads have proved rather too successful since they eat almost anything, produce vast numbers of eggs (up to 30,000 per clutch) and do not have any serious predators in Australia. At night they can often be seen sitting under streetlights or garden lights, plucking flying insects out of the air.

BATTY SUPERSTITIONS

Despite their sometimes mysterious and sinister image, bats are in fact inoffensive animals, which are keen to avoid their human neighbours. They prefer to roost in modern, clean houses rather than dusty, draughty old ones. They are incredibly clean and usually quiet. Long-eared bats like these have the longest ears relative to their body size of any mammal. They use their sensitive ears to pick up the echoes of high-pitched sounds they make. This is called 'echolocation' and helps most bats to navigate and find food.

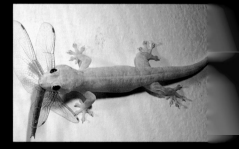

LUCKY GECKOS

In tropical countries, the sound of a gecko in the bedroom at night is a welcome one because it is there to catch insects. In Bangkok, it is supposed to be an especially good sign if a gecko happens to be uttering its cry when a baby is born. Geckos have a kind of suction pad under their toes to help them scurry up and down the walls, and upside-down across the ceiling – lucky for the geckos, less lucky for their prey.

HOUSE PARTY

Did you know that about one million dust mites live in an ordinary single bed? Or that book lice feed on the tiny moulds that grow on the pages of books or under wallpaper? These are just two of the many creatures that lurk unseen in the hidden corners of our homes – on walls, or in wardrobes, carpets, curtains and kitchen cupboards. Many of them are tiny, or microscopic, but a few, such as bats in the loft or mice under the floorboards, are larger, noisier and more obvious. Some of them would once have lived in caves or big holes in trees but prefer the warmth of our homes, with their built-in food supply. The larvae of many moths and beetles munch their way through our food, clothes, curtains and carpets. They include clothes moths, meal moths, flour beetles, bacon beetles, leather beetles, grain weevils and carpet beetles. Some of these insects find their way into our homes from the nests of birds, rodents and wasps, which are built in and around human habitats.

DUST FOR DINNER

Billions of microscopic dust mites chomp away on the bits of dead skin that flake off our bodies. Much of the dust in our homes is made up of human skin! Dust mites are so small you cannot see them and no one knew they were there until about 30 years ago. Some people are allergic to dust mite droppings. They sniff and sneeze and even get asthma if they breathe in too many of them.

YUMMY CARPETS

Carpet beetle larvae are covered with hairs so are called woolly bears. They feed on woollen textiles, hair and feathers. Adult females lay their eggs in places where there will be food for the larvae. In the wild, the eggs are laid in the nests of mice and birds. Adult carpet beetles fly around outside during the summer and feed on nectar and pollen. They often find their way indoors.

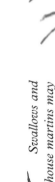

Swallows and house martins may nest under the gutters of houses.

SWALLOWS

ANIMAL LODGERS

The artificial habitats in our homes are similar to many natural ones – walls are like cliffs, attics and cellars are like caves, chimney pots are like tall trees and wooden furniture is like the fallen logs in a forest. Even though we may not be aware of it, our homes are full of uninvited guests. Some can cause problems by carrying diseases or destroying the structure of our homes and the things in them. Others, such as spiders and geckos, are useful because they eat unwanted insects.

STORKS

Bats are safe from predators in the attic. Young bats can practise flying there too.

BATS

Wasps may hang their paper nests from attic beams.

WASPS

COCKROACH SURVIVAL

Cockroaches are mainly tropical insects that have travelled all over the world with people. They probably could not survive in cooler countries outside towns and cities. Cockroaches are active at night and spend the day hidden in warm places, such as ovens or radiators, although they have been found in televisions, clocks, telephones and on the backs of fridges. They eat almost anything, including glue, paper, soap, shoe polish and ink and can exist without food for up to three months. Cockroaches have to keep clean to preserve their waxy coating, which stops them from drying out in centrally-heated homes. But they can spread bacteria that is harmful to humans.

TASTY CLOTHES

The larvae of clothes moths feed on anything made from animal or plant fibres, such as woollens, silks and cottons. They will also feed on flour, meat and dead insects. Clothes moths originally came from warmer parts of the world and do not live outside in cooler, temperate countries. They have been decreasing as more synthetic materials have been used to make clothes, and because our homes are cleaned more efficiently and have become drier with better heating.

BITING BUGS

Bedbugs are about 6 mm (¼ inch) long and are big enough to see easily. They jab their piercing mouthparts into a victim and suck up their blood. In about ten minutes, an adult bed bug can suck up to seven times its own weight in blood. In human beings, each jab of a bed bug leaves a red, itchy spot. Bed bugs probably came originally from Asia but have now spread to all parts of the world. They need a warm, dry climate, and spread to northern parts of the world once buildings started to be well heated.

Geckos cling to walls and ceilings and hunt insects.

SPIDERS

Spiders are useful house guests who stalk, snare and ambush insects for breakfast, lunch and dinner.

WOODWORM

The larvae of woodworm beetles can reduce furniture to dust.

GECKOS

HOUSEFLIES

Houseflies visit dung, carrion and offal of all kinds and can carry diseases.

FLEAS

Cat fleas suck a cat's blood and will bite humans too.

SILVERFISH

Silverfish are often found in kitchens, searching for sugary and starchy foods.

HOUSE MICE

House mice live in attics, under floors and in gaps in brickwork, gnawing through wooden partitions to find food.

FOXES

Foxes may nest in cellars or under the floorboards.

ON THE ROAD

The roads that criss-cross our towns and cities can be useful as corridors, allowing animals to move from one area to another. They can also provide feeding grounds for insects and small seed-eating birds, as well as hunting birds, such as kestrels and owls, or scavengers such as crows, magpies and jackdaws. But, on the whole, they are polluted and dangerous for animals, especially slow-moving ones, such as toads that need to cross roads to reach their breeding ponds, or low-flying birds, such as blackbirds. Badgers suffer too, because roads may cut across the traditional tracks they follow from sett to sett. The usual defences of many animals are useless against cars and trucks – hedgehogs roll up into a ball and rely on their spines for protection; deer and rabbits freeze if they think running is too risky. Sometimes, animals are protected by people who set up special crossing points on roads.

LOOK-OUT POINT

A kestrel perches on a motorway bridge, keeping a sharp lookout for small birds or rodents next to the road. Kestrels seem to be unconcerned by the traffic thundering along beneath them. They are the only birds that can truly hover in the air, keeping their head still to see better. Grassy roadside verges where small animals have little chance to hide provide kestrels with good hunting.

ANIMAL CROSSINGS

Specially designed signs aim to draw drivers' attention to the possibility of animals on the road, rather like the warning signs showing children outside schools. The hope is that the drivers will slow down and take more care once they see the signs. People sometimes stand by the side of the road to help toads get across the roads safely as they migrate to their breeding grounds at night.

KOALA WALKABOUT

This koala has not chosen a good spot for watching the traffic. Although koalas spend much of their time in the trees, they often come to the ground where they can run. They are also excellent swimmers. Koalas usually occupy areas of about 3–4 hectares (7–10 acres) but have been recorded walking 30 km (18 miles) or more.

ROAD CASUALTIES

This fox is yet another victim of a speeding car. Snakes are often killed when they come out to lie on a warm road surface. Every road-user is unfortunately familiar with animals seen flattened on the road or lying battered at the edge. Even if an animal is only injured, it may die later from the shock of the accident or be too badly injured to survive in the wild.

TURTLE TRUCK

With an enormous truck speeding towards it only a few metres away, a slow-moving turtle has little chance of crossing the road safely. Its strong shell was not designed to withstand such a powerful crushing force. Semi-terrestrial turtles live both in water and on land and eat both plants and animal food.

THE CLEAN-UP CREWS

RUBBISH RATS

Rats thrive in the dirtiest parts of town, which include rubbish tips. Rats in the Italian city of Pisa were once deprived of their rubbish-tip food when a new rubbish incinerator was built. They responded by swarming into the city centre, only leaving when refuse was delivered from a neighbouring town. Rats are intelligent, cunning survivors, but they cause damage in towns, as well as spreading diseases.

From household rubbish left outside our homes to rubbish left on the streets or dumped in large landfill sites, the food we throw away feeds a large number of different urban animals and winged scavengers. As the rubbish decomposes, it releases warmth which attracts indoor scavengers, like cockroaches and house crickets, as well as mice in the winter. Reptiles such as grass snakes, lizards and slowworms may also use the internal warmth of a rubbish tip. The large number of rubbish-dwelling invertebrates includes dung flies, bluebottles, houseflies, hoverflies, owl midges, spiders, bees, earthworms, roundworms and springtails. All these creatures act as natural recyclers, making good use of the rubbish we throw away.

GREEDY GULLS

The harsh sound of gulls squabbling over juicy bits of rubbish is a noisy reminder of the important role scavengers play in the natural world. These gulls no longer live by the sea and instead spend most of the year feeding at rubbish tips. They migrate to the coast only to breed. The gulls are tough, aggressive and expert at finding tasty morsels among the rubbish. Some species even rob other gulls of their food. Common gulls get almost all of their own food by robbing black-headed gulls.

BEAR VISITORS

In the autumn, large numbers of polar bears pass by a town called Churchill, in Canada, on their way to reach their hunting grounds. The bears are hungry after spending summer on land, where there are no seals for them to hunt. They find the rubbish dump of Churchill particularly attractive. The bears are a serious hazard to the people of Churchill, however, since they are very strong and unpredictable.

RACCOON PROOF?

So-called 'raccoon proof' rubbish bins do little to prevent racoons stealing rubbish and making a mess. They can use their front paws to unscrew lids or pull tops from bottles. They have even been known to lift a door latch, walk into a kitchen, open a refrigerator and help themselves to the contents.

SCAVENGER STORK

Marabou storks of Africa obtain most of their food by scavenging and are often attracted to human rubbish tips. They need over 700 g (24 oz) of food each day and also scavenge at lion kills, where they compete with vultures and hyenas for food. Their size and large bills help them to steal bits of food from nearby vultures. Here they are joined by some baboons who are hoping to find an easy meal.

WOOLLY RECYCLERS

People do throw away a lot of food, which makes a tasty free meal for many animals. These Welsh sheep may not be the most common visitors to rubbish dumps but they are helping to recycle some of our rubbish. This is useful as there is too much human rubbish and not enough places for it to go. Rubbish can contain sharp or broken objects though, which can injure both animals and people sorting through the leftovers.

URBAN WETLANDS

E ven though many towns and cities are built near rivers and streams, it is often the man-made waterways of canals, reservoirs, old gravel pits, and park ponds that are more useful for wildlife. Reservoirs are particularly important for migrating wildfowl. Slow-moving canal waters shelter pond creatures, such as frogs, pond skaters, water voles and moorhens. Bridges and other buildings by canals provide roosting sites for bats. Ponds are fascinating mini-ecosystems for a variety of invertebrates, as well as frogs, newts and fish. Larger animals such as foxes and hedgehogs may drink from them. Spectacular looking kingfishers are also sometimes seen along waterways right in the middle of towns.

SPINNING BEETLES

On the surface of still or slow-moving waters, whirligig beetles spin around in small groups. Most of their legs are flattened and have small hairs for swimming. The eyes are divided into two parts, the top part for seeing in the air and the bottom part for seeing under the water. Adult whirligig beetles feed mainly on insects that have fallen onto the surface of the water. To survive cold winter temperatures, the whirligigs bury themselves in the mud.

SLOW-MOVER

Unlike most water snails, which eat only plants, the great pond snail also eats decaying animals, fish eggs and even small fish. It is common in large ponds in Britain and Europe and has also become established in Australia, Asia and the middle states of the USA. Great pond snails can obtain oxygen from the air using a simple lung and remain underwater for long periods in well-oxygenated waters.

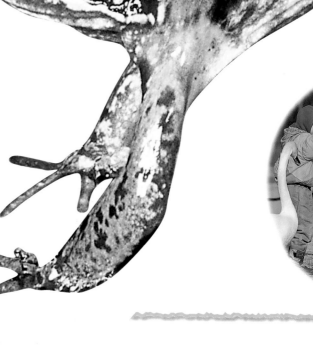

MOSQUITO EMERGENCE

Mosquito larvae must live in water, whether it is a pond or a metal can full of water. In the United States, they are called 'wrigglers'. They hang upside-down from the surface of the water, breathing air through a tube. Eventually, they turn into pupae, which stretch out on the surface when the adult is ready to emerge. The adult stretches upwards until the ends of its long legs slip out of the pupa and its body can drop forwards onto the surface of the water (left). After resting for a short time, the mosquito flies away.

Only the females suck blood – they need a meal of blood before they can lay their eggs. The males are nectar-feeders.

SHY FROG

Adult frogs are very shy and leap into the water at the first sign of danger. Their long shape and powerful back legs with webbed toes, help them to swim fast. Frogs mate and lay their eggs in the water. The jelly around the eggs helps to keep them warm and protects the eggs from damage caused by other animals or the movement of the water. The eggs hatch into tiny tadpoles, which have no legs and breathe through gills. Eventually, they develop into frogs, with legs and lungs, and hop out of the water onto land.

NEWT DANCE

In spring, the male great crested newt develops a high crest along his back and tail and turns bright orange-red underneath. He produces secretions from special glands to attract a mate. The female lays up to 300 eggs, which she wraps individually in the leaves of water plants. When handled, this newt gives out a nasty fluid.

EXTRA FOOD

Waterfowl, such as these swans, benefit from the extra food people bring for them. But they can also be harmed by polluted waters or injured by rubbish, such as plastic bags and tins. Swans sometimes die after becoming entangled in fishing lines or by swallowing the lead fishing weights along with the stones they take in to help them grind up their food. As the lead is ground up in the swans' stomach, it slowly poisons the swans. Non-toxic alternatives to lead weights have saved many swans from this unpleasant fate.

SPECIAL JOURNEYS

Changes in the food supply or a change of season may force some urban animals to embark on long migration journeys. One swallow was recorded flying from Johannesburg to Leninsk-Kuznetskiy in Russia, a distance of some 12,000 km (7,500 miles), in just 34 days. Other urban visitors, such as moose, wander over much smaller distances, but their journeys are also based on the need to find food. The fruit bats of the tropics make regular migration journeys to find ripe fruit. Migrating animals find their way by using instinctive knowledge, physical landmarks, the Earth's magnetic field, sounds, smells and the position of the Sun, Moon and stars. Feral pigeons have a reputation for their homing skills, but they actually find their home roost from relatively small distances – up to about 160 km (100 miles).

FRUITFUL SEARCH

Most fruit bats live in large groups. In Kampala, Uganda, hundreds of thousands of bats hang from trees during the day-time. Fruit bats often migrate in search of ripening fruit. For instance, the grey-headed fruit bat of Australia moves about in search of wild figs. Australian flying foxes migrate from Queensland to New South Wales, often doing considerable damage to fruit trees in northern and eastern Australia. Fruit bats also migrate to South Africa during the southern summer and fly northwards down the Nile in the rainy season.

ROUTE CHANGES

People have changed the migration habits of the Canada goose, which used to breed in the Alaskan summer and fly south to the Gulf of Mexico for the winter. Many geese now remain in city parks all year round waiting to be fed by people. Thousands of geese also stay in wildlife refuges in the USA, rather than flying further south. Geese can cause hygiene problems in parks because of the huge amount of waste they produce. A flock of 300 geese can produce a tonne of waste in four days.

CAN SOMEONE TAKE MY ORDER?

This moose has obviously taken a liking to fast food! During the warmer seasons, moose wander over a vast area of the countryside and sometimes end up in cities. In the winter, they tend to come together and retire to some sheltered area, where they remain until the warmer weather returns in spring. The promise of food may also draw them to cities in winter.

SOARING STORKS

White storks migrate from Europe into Africa to avoid the cold European winter, returning year after year to their favourite chimney pots and rooftops to build their enormous nests. Migrating flocks of storks – sometimes hundreds strong – are a spectacular sight on their autumn migrations as they soar on the warm thermals rising over cities such as Istanbul and Gibraltar. They will not fly over large expanses of water where there are no thermals on which they can glide.

SWALLOW SURVIVAL

European swallows spend half the year in Europe and half the year in Africa. In the autumn, they leave behind the cold winter weather and the shortage of insect food and fly south to a relatively warm and safe environment in Africa. In spring, they fly north again to Europe, where there are long hours of daylight and large amounts of food – two advantages when raising their young. On their migration journeys, swallows may cover as much as 300 km (186 miles) a day, at a speed of over 70 km/h (43 mph).

HITCH-HIKERS

Some urban animals do not choose to make their journeys. They are carried round the world on ships or planes by accident. This tree frog might very well find itself transported to a new home on a ship, as the bananas are shipped from a tropical country to a cooler one. Spiders are often transported like this, including the various 'banana spiders', such as *Heteropoda venatoria*. Spiders also travel with bunches of grapes because they were busy feeding on grape pests when the grapes were harvested.

NESTS, EGGS & YOUNG

PAPER NEST

Wasps build truly amazing nests of papier-mâché made from chewed-up wood. The paper nest is made up of eight or more layers of six-sided cells, which are joined to the layers above by pillars of paper. The queen wasp lays eggs in the cells, which hatch into worker wasps. She has to glue the eggs into the cells to stop them falling out. At the end of the summer, workers make larger 'royal cells' in which to raise new queens. The whole nest is covered with several layers of wasp paper.

Birds, insects, frogs, toads, snakes and mammals all find safe places to build their nests and raise their young in our homes, gardens, parks and offices. The fact that some people put out food for town and city creatures is a real help for busy animal parents struggling to fill the ever-hungry mouths of their offspring. Birds, in particular, often choose the oddest spots for their nests, from old vacuum cleaners and empty paint pots to mail boxes and aircraft. A mallard duck even built her nest in a window box on the seventh floor of a block of flats. She had to rely on a human helper to carry her ducklings down to the lake below. Urban birds make use of some unusual nesting materials, such as crisp packets, plastic footballs, tennis rackets and telephone wire. Wasps also build their nests in awkward places, such as porches, conservatories or even under beds.

UGLY DUCKLINGS

A housing estate was built near the breeding grounds of this swan, so it now has to take the cygnets (its young) across the road instead of grass to get to water. Mute swans usually have four to seven young grey cygnets, which cannot fly until they are four-and-a-half months old. In the Middle Ages, swan meat, especially that of the cygnets, was highly prized as a source of food. Enormous numbers were eaten at royal banquets. At Christmas in 1251, Henry III of England collected 125 swans for the festive celebrations.

SNAKE INCUBATORS

Grass snakes often lay their eggs in garden compost heaps. The warmth given off by the rotting vegetation helps the embryos in the eggs to develop fast enough to survive their first winter. As well as compost heaps, grass snakes have been known to lay their eggs in manure heaps, piles of sawdust and holes in the walls of bakeries, where the ovens keep the building very warm.

EGG CARRIER

The male midwife toad, found in western European gardens, is a caring parent. He winds a string of 35–50 eggs around his back legs and carries them around for protection. He keeps the eggs moist by dipping them in shallow pools or puddles from time to time. After about three weeks, the male takes his eggs to water, where they hatch into tadpoles and complete their development into adult toads.

TROUSER NEST

A pair of trousers provides a handy nesting place for this wren, which has hungry youngsters to feed. Birds that are willing to nest close to people can use nest sites that other competitors may not be bold enough to use. People may also help to stop some predators from attacking the nest and stealing the young.

ILLUMINATED NEST

This house sparrow has made its nest in a street lamp in Bahrain. Sparrows build untidy nests of grass and straw, lined with feathers. They will often rob other birds, such as pigeons or ducks, of their feathers. Hen sparrows lay four or five whitish eggs, often in other sparrows' nests. Eggs are incubated for about two weeks and the nestlings (young) develop wings in about another two weeks. Some young nestlings fall out of their nests onto pavements below, before they are able to fly.

BLOWING BUBBLES

Froghoppers are insect bugs that suck the sap from plants. They get their name from the way they hop about like tiny frogs. Adults can fly away from danger, but nymphs (the young) cannot, so they protect themselves by living in blobs of white froth. The nymphs make the froth by blowing air into a sticky fluid that comes out of the rear end of the body. The froth also helps to stop the nymph from drying out.

DISCOVERING URBAN WILDLIFE

People have only been living in cities for some 5,000 years, so this is a fairly new habitat for wildlife. But, unlike other wildlife habitats, it is growing rapidly. By the year 2020, 80 per cent of people will be living in towns and cities. We need to understand more about how urban animals survive if we are to encourage those animals that cause us no harm and control those that do. When we encourage urban animals to live in our towns and cities, it is inevitable that some of the popular species, such as butterflies and birds, will be eaten by unpopular ones, such as magpies and toads. This is all part of the balance of nature, even in an artificial urban setting. The four best ways to help urban animals are to provide shelter, homes, food and water. Water is vital, both during summer droughts and winter frosts, and can be as small as a pan of water on a balcony or as large as a pond in a garden or city park.

ROADSIDE RESERVES

The grassy verges at the side of roads can become useful nature reserves if the grass and flowers are allowed to grow. This Texas roadside is filled with wild flowers, which attract insects, and the insects, in turn, attract birds. Small mammals, such as mice and voles, can feed on seeds, roots and shoots in these grassy areas. Although the animals have to put up with the traffic fumes and noise, they are not usually disturbed by people whizzing past in their cars, unaware of the living world so near their tyres.

BEE USEFUL

Some people in smaller towns manage to keep bees in their gardens. This beekeeper is checking on the well-being of the honeybees in one of his hives. Bees are excellent for gardens as they pollinate flowers while collecting nectar and pollen to feed their larvae. Back in the hive, they change the nectar into honey, which the beekeeper can eat.

FREE FOOD

These rainbow lorikeets are feeding in a backyard in eastern Australia. People who feed birds in their gardens help them to survive and are rewarded by wonderful close-up views of the birds themselves. In countries colder than Australia, free food in the backyard or garden can be a real lifesaver in the winter, especially for small birds that need to eat a lot of food to keep warm.

CLEARING UP

Many areas of waste ground in cities, even small ones, can provide valuable habitats for wild animals, but only if unpolluted. These children are clearing up a wild patch of ground in London to make it safe for wildlife. Making things too neat and tidy both disturbs and discourages wild animals though. Overgrown corners, with piles of old logs and stones provide ideal places for animals to rest and hibernate. The greater the variety of native plants, including weeds, the greater the variety of insects and birds that can feed and shelter there.

FINDING OUT MORE

To plan the best way to help urban animals, it is important to know which animals are visiting our urban habitat, how many of them there are and where they are living. Then, any changes in populations can be recorded, problems avoided, and help given to animals where it is most needed. Information gathered by ordinary people identifying the birds on their streets and in their gardens can be very helpful to conservationists, although it is unnecessary, and harmful, to catch the birds! A pair of binoculars and a good bird book is all you need.

FEEDING BIRDS

If you do feed the birds, try to use a variety of different foods, such as peanuts, sunflower seeds, cheese, currants, bits of bacon rind, half coconuts, bread crusts and biscuit crumbs. You can offer food in a variety of ways – on a table for starlings, sparrows and robins; in a hanging container for tits, woodpeckers, siskins and nuthatches; and on the ground for thrushes, dunnocks and blackbirds. It is also a good idea to use a number of different places for the feeding stations. This makes it more difficult for cats to attack and gives the less aggressive birds a chance to feed. It also prevents the build-up of stale food, which might attract rats.

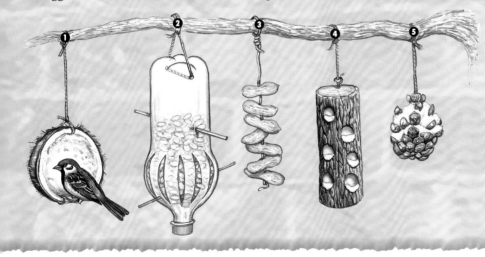

HERE ARE DIFFERENT TYPES OF BIRDFEEDERS YOU CAN MAKE YOURSELF.

1 Half a coconut
2 Peanuts or bird seed in a bottle or net
3 Peanuts hung on string or wire
4 Peanuts or fat in holes in a log
5 Pine cone filled with melted fat

GLOSSARY

Domestic An animal that is tame and kept by humans.

Echolocation A way of locating objects by sending out sound waves and listening to the echo that comes back.

Ecosystem A community of living and non-living things which depend on each other for mutual survival.

Feral A once domesticated animal that has returned to the wild.

Hibernation The time when some animals go into a deep sleep for the winter, living off the fat stored in their bodies.

Invertebrate An animal that does not have a backbone.

Marsupial Mammals with pouches on their front, which baby marsupials live in when they are first born.

Migration The movement of animals from one habitat to another according to the seasons.

Moult When an animal sheds its old feathers, hair or skin to make way for new growth.

Roost A place, usually a high perch, where birds go to rest and sleep.

ACKNOWLEDGEMENTS

We would like to thank: Helen Wire and Elizabeth Wiggans for their assistance. Artwork by Peter Bull Art Studio.

Copyright © 2009 *ticktock* Entertainment Ltd

First published in Great Britain by *ticktock* Media Ltd, Kent TN1 2DP, U.K.

This edition published in 2012 by PAPP International Inc., 177 Merizzi Street, Montreal (Quebec) H4T 1Y3 Canada.

All rights reserved. No part of this publication may be reproduced, stored in a retrieval system, or transmitted in any form or by any means electronic, mechanical, photocopying, recording or otherwise, without prior written permission of the copyright owner.

A CIP catalogue record for this book is available from the British Library.

ISBN 978 177066 3145

Picture research by Image Select. Printed in China.

Picture Credits: t=top, b=bottom, c=centre, l=left, r=right, OFC=outside front cover, OBC=outside back cover, IFC=inside front cover

Bruce Coleman Collection; 8/9t, 10b, 11tr, 12/13c, 13b, 14l, 20/21t, 22ct, 24bl, 27tr. Chris Fairclough; 21bl. Heather Angel; 15br, 16/17b, 27bl, 30tl. Image Bank; 15t, 16cl & 32, 21br, 30bl. NHPA; 13r. Oxford Scientific Films; IFC, 2/3t, 2l, 3br, 3cr, 3t, 4bl, 4tl, 4/5b, 5tr, 5ct, 6l, 6br, 6/7t, 7tr, 7br, 9tr, 8bl, 9cl, 8tl, 9cr, 10tl, 10/11c, 11cr, 12tl, 14ct, 15c, 16tl, 17tr, 17cr, 17tl, 18/19c, 18/19t, 19c, 19tr, 20bl, 20br, 20tl, 22/23b, 23tr, 23cr, 23br, 24tl, 24/25b, 24/25c, 24/25t, 25br, 27cr, 26t, 26/27c, 29cl, 28bl, 28/29t, 29b, 28tl, 29cr, 29tr, 30/31t, 30br. OBC (both). Shutterstock; OFC. Survival Anglia; 5tl. Tony Stone Images; 7cr, 18tl, 22l, 26l, 30cr.

Every effort has been made to trace the copyright holders and we apologise in advance for anyunintentional omissions. We would be pleased to insert the appropriate acknowledgement in anysubsequent edition of this publication.